Dear Current Occupant

DEAR CURRENT OCCUPANT

A MEMOIR

CHELENE KNIGHT

Book*hug 2018 | ESSAIS NO. 5

The photographs on page 8 and on pages 54–70 are by Jade Melnychuk / jade creativeco.com. Used with permission.

Map Illustration on page 53 by Jesse Huisken.

 Canada Council **Conseil des Arts** Funded by the Financé par le | Canadä
for the Arts du Canada Government gouvernement
of Canada du Canada

 ONTARIO ARTS COUNCIL
CONSEIL DES ARTS DE L'ONTARIO
an Ontario government agency
un organisme du gouvernement de l'Ontario

The production of this book was made possible through the generous assistance of the Canada Council for the Arts and the Ontario Arts Council. Book*hug also acknowledges the support of the Government of Canada through the Canada Book Fund and the Government of Ontario through the Ontario Book Publishing Tax Credit and the Ontario Book Fund.

Book*hug acknowledges the land on which it operates. For thousands of years it has been the traditional land of the Huron-Wendat, the Seneca, and, most recently, the Mississaugas of the Credit River. Today, this meeting place is still the home to many Indigenous people from across Turtle Island, and we are grateful to have the opportunity to work on this land.

LIBRARY AND ARCHIVES CANADA CATALOGUING IN PUBLICATION

Knight, Chelene, 1981-, author
    Dear current occupant : a memoir / Chelene Knight.

Issued in print and electronic formats.
ISBN 978-1-77166-390-8 (softcover).--ISBN 978-1-77166-391-5 (HTML).--
ISBN 978-1-77166-392-2 (PDF).--ISBN 978-1-77166-393-9 (Kindle)

    1. Creative nonfiction, Canadian (English). 2. Knight, Chelene, 1981-. I. Title.

PS8621.N53D43 2018   C818'.603   C2017-908060-1
                                               C2017-908061-X

for Adelaide Riordan
1936–2017

"I dream loud in this house. I pull my bed
down from that wall, and I fall to my knees
next to it to question this shelter.
I sleep while a limp breeze dies at the window,
waking to dawn tangled with my dust.
This is my house."

—Patricia Smith, "Only Everything I Own"

Clark Drive

Contents

Prologue

15   I think about all the houses

17   This is for the teachers

19   Grade six

20   Waiting out front of the school to be picked up was torture

21   When the smoke cleared

22   Mama

Dear Current Occupant: Part One

27   House with the sign in the window

29   Origami house with the handmade roof

30   Duplex near Fraser Street with the picture books in the closet

31   Letter to Santa

32   House with the green door on East 12th Avenue

33   Basement suite on Earles Street

35   Apartment above the East Indian sweet shop just off 49th

36   Palms Motel, Kingsway

37   House we all shared on Forgotten Street

38   Two-toned red-and-white brick house on 41st behind the church

Witness Statements

43   I didn't have a father

44   Pack your things

45   apartment 301 near the low track

46   white house where some family lived upstairs

47   most holidays

48   like a lion in the trees

49   of the last house I remember

cracks in the sidewalk

53	Walking tour, a map
54	Broadway and Commercial
54	41st Avenue between Victoria and Elliott, back
55	Clark Drive 2
55	Clark Drive 3
56	East 12th Avenue (off Commercial)
57	41st Avenue between Wales and Clarendon
58	East 12th between Windsor and Fraser, back alley
59	East 12th between Windsor and Fraser, back alley
60	Clark Drive traffic
60	East 12th between Windsor and Fraser, front door
61	East 13th Avenue, attic
62	East 13th Avenue, front
63	East 41st between Victoria and Elliott
64	Broadway and Commercial, back
64	East 41st between Victoria and Elliott, roof
65	Fraser and 13th
65	Kingsway and Fraser
66	Kingsway Hotel
66	Kingsway Hotel, side view
67	View from front window of East 12th
68	Gate, white house
69	Clark Drive intersection
70	Mailboxes

Dear Current Occupant: Part Two

73   She's at the recovery house for the third time

74   Apartment on Clark Drive above the convenience store

75   For Uncle Eugene

76   Owl House Women and Children's Shelter

77   The room in the attic of the oldest place we've stayed

78   Pink building, Broadway and 12th

79   House with the attic apartment where kittens disappear

80   Neighbour, this is for your daughter

81   One-room apartment above the grocery store

82   Third-floor corner unit apartment, East Broadway

83   House where I accidentally dyed my hair blond

84   Of every yard I didn't have

Mirror Talk

87   let your hair down

88   the eyes have it

89   *these hands*

90   these lips taste water

Notices of Termination

93   the occupants of these suites must adhere to the following rules

94   damage noted

95   I broke the rules on purpose

96   someone slashed the tops off coconuts so we could drink the milk

97   Miss Parker

104   Lay your head on my pillow

epilogue

109   mama, you need to know some things

Endnotes

115   home
117   black and female while writing
120   never sure how the word *Dad*
123   the cracks in the narrative

Acknowledgements

127   Thank-yous
129   Notes

131   Chelene Knight

Prologue

I think about all the houses and I try to remember the little details—I used to cough from the mixed fumes in the air, while Mama's cigarette smoke and pine cleaner pinned my eyelids to my brows. I try to remember the way I'd only eat a handful of things. I was picky. I was skinny. My hair was big but I had *good* hair. I had thin wrists and tiny ankles. I kept an inventory of my things. I was light-skinned. Everyone saw me from the outside in. I'd never wear my hair down.

There were so many houses. Never mine, never ours. These houses—carpets, floors, cupboards, missing closet doors, light bulbs, faucets, shelves, bathrooms, shower curtains, phone cords—constantly changing. Vancouver Eastside. Let me count the times the front door would slam in the middle of the night and the hinges squeak, lost in the breath of men… Mama's visitors would come and go, never staying long enough to remember my name. My name, the skin-crawling sensation of a voice asking something, and then, "No, that's my daughter."

Twenty or thirty houses. Many close together, some on the same block. I loved this city. Walk with me: Fraser, Kingsway, Clark, East 12th, Commercial, Broadway, Woodlands, Earles, 49th. Hold your things close. Sometimes we had to leave at a moment's notice, taking only what we could carry and leaving behind what we couldn't. We filled shopping carts, baskets, boxes, garbage bags, backpacks. I noticed the colour of paint, walls, and doors. I took shelter in the frames of small spaces I thought no one would see.

The cracks in the sidewalk—

I wanted to crawl in. It wasn't all bad: like the days I fell into books. Reading about being someone else. In each of these houses I spent my days writing about being someplace where I could mouth the word *home* and mean it. I wanted a corner nook where I could line my books along a wide windowsill. I wanted a large armchair, tall enough that my legs would swing and hover above a tiled floor. I'd be safe. I could settle into my brother's laughter at jokes neither of us understood. I'd dream of days spent listening to music. I'd lie on my bed, turn up the radio, and close my eyes. Music played just for me.

I was eleven when I realized there could be music woven into words. Rhythms and cadence shifted in between colons and dashes. I was eleven when my teacher told me to sing loud. I was eleven when I realized I had a voice, and that everyone deserved to be heard. I wanted to sing loud. When I turned twelve, one of my classmates called me a nigger. It was at that moment I learned how to open my mouth and speak.

"Sing loud," she said. This blond white woman balancing in three-inch heels hovered over me. Her wide body created a criss-cross design of shadow and light.

"Sing loud," she said.

She pulled me into the dim cloakroom, where yellow, red, green, and brown raincoats lined the wall like infantry. I stood there in the dark of her dress. She placed the palm of her hand on my shoulder. "Never let anyone say that to you again. Don't let anyone dull your shine."

I stood there confused, quiet. She lowered one knee to the ground, and her gaze met mine. I stuck my index finger inside my tightly sculpted hair bun, searching eagerly for scalp.

"Why, miss?" I continued to scratch inside my hair bun.

"Because you're going to grow up to be a strong Black woman. Hasn't anyone ever told you that?"

I remember that day in that cloakroom. I never wanted to be a woman. I never wanted to be a Black woman because I had no idea how.

This is for the teachers. Growing up, I never had a Black teacher. I never had a Black woman teacher. I never had a Black or mixed-race teacher. I never had a Black or mixed-race woman teacher who understood what it was like to grow up poor, to live with a mother who struggled with addiction and sex work, or be a child forced to carry the weight of a low-functioning adult on her shoulders while trying to get an education. And I never once questioned this. Until now.

Why does this matter? Teachers hold a lot of power. Teachers are gatekeepers. I will not dance around this. How can a little Black girl be guaranteed she's offered the same opportunities as all the other children in her classes? We've seen the movies that now centre around this very question, but is that enough? How do they challenge her, support her, teach her? How do teachers make sure that girl can sit calm at her desk without the worry that she isn't good enough, and that what she has to say isn't good enough? How do they guarantee that her voice will be heard? All of these questions and thoughts formed twenty-five years later. Now, as an adult, a mother, a professional writer, and an editor, I can see the cracks in the narrative.

Looking back at my younger self, I wonder what would have changed for me had I ever been handed a book written by a Black female author. How might that have influenced my life? A big question. Dionne Brand, Jamaica Kincaid, Toni Morrison, Esi Edugyan, Cecily Nicholson, to name just a few. What are the reasons names like these never crossed my desk?

Society puts so much blame on the parents. It's the parents' job to teach their children everything they need to know, and this is true to some extent. But let's break this down a bit: if a child spends eight hours a day, five days a week, for fifteen years of their life, sitting at a desk listening to "teachers," then how much of the responsibility falls to these teachers?

Most people may read this book and think, wow, that's really sad, or they may say they feel bad that a little girl experienced these things. But that's not the purpose of this book. It took me twenty-five years to figure out that my mother saved my life. And even though it was most likely not her intention, she showed me what could happen if I didn't have a dream. She showed me what could happen if I didn't work hard. She showed me what could happen if I let the wrong people in, or left the door open for too long. Maybe, for me, she was the only one who could do that.

Maybe she was the real gatekeeper.

So yes, teachers are gatekeepers. Teachers hold a lot of power, and that responsibility will never change. Growing up, I never had a Black teacher. I never had a Black woman teacher. I never had a Black or mixed-race teacher. I had a mother.

Grade six. Nineteen ninety-two. I had this teacher, Mrs. McCloud. I was eleven years old. She said I was a writer. She said these words. I filled up class journals. One per month. Everyone else had one for the entire year. She asked me to read my short stories in front of the class. She sat at her desk and ran a thin blue comb through her triangular short blond hair. With the paper in front of my face, I mumbled through them. I looked over at her, her short triangular hair, large-framed body, small eyes. Small smiling eyes. She saw me in the basement cafeteria sitting with friends who had their lunches splayed out across the folding linoleum tables: orange slices, sandwiches with iceberg lettuce and thick-sliced tomato. Cheese. Bananas only slightly bruised. Peanut butter and jelly. I sat there. Lips permanently pursed around the straw of my grape-flavoured juice box. Hair pulled back tight. Headband with a plastic white teddy bear on the side. Pink shirt with a scoop neck. She walked over to me. Put her hand on my shoulder, her blue eyes bigger than I'd ever seen them. She said nothing. She eased her hand down to the middle of my back, right between my shoulder blades. With her other hand she motioned for me to stand up. I stood up. We walked away from the table with the splayed lunches over to the hot-lunch line. We stood there in silence. The line moved. We moved. Silence stayed still. My heart pounded. She said nothing. We got to the front of the line to pay. I looked up at her. She motioned for me to keep walking. I did. She looked at the cafeteria cashier with her small but big eyes. Whispered something. The cafeteria cashier nodded in response. I walked back over to the linoleum table with the splayed lunches and added mine to the mix. I sat down with my friends. We picked up where we had left off, talking about New Kids on the Block. I looked up to see if Mrs. McCloud was there. She wasn't.

Waiting out front of the school to be picked up was torture. I never knew how long I'd stand there. I never knew if Mama would show up or if she would send one of her friends—or no one. I found ways to occupy myself. I sat on the metal pole of the schoolyard fence, balancing my third-grade math textbook on the boniness of my knees. The equations with the brackets kept my mind spinning like bike spokes, and I loved the way this felt. The wind was always the first thing I noticed. Its coolness, the sweetness, the changing smell of the wind kept me company every day at 3:00 p.m. I pulled those tiny white-and-yellow buttercup flowers from the grass. I slit the thin stems of each one with the jagged nail of my thumb. I slipped the bottom tip of one flower into the next. I did this over and over until I had a chain of sliced buttercups as tall as me. I took my buttercup chain and raised it above my head and closed my eyes. I searched for the top of my tightly pulled hair bun and wrapped and wrapped and wrapped the chain around my hair. I couldn't see it but I felt like a queen. I lifted my neck and my head felt weightless.

When the smoke cleared I saw her eyes—glassy and sad. She blinked in slow motion through the clouds of thick grey. Maybe she forgot I was sitting there on that small floral couch. Her, in the brown armchair, legs crossed. Her head and shoulders barely visible in that fog. Maybe she didn't see me through the smoke. Or maybe she didn't care. Either way, I watched her. The charred black around her eyes melted into smudges under her lids. This was the chapter about her I wish I could rewrite. This was the part I wish never happened. She should have had the chance to show the world the woman *I* saw. She was my mother.

This was the chapter where she got bit by the poisonous snake. This was the chapter where she was dreaming and running in slow motion but never fast enough to escape its grip. Its jaws widened, then clenched firmly around her neck. This was the chapter where you knew as soon as you turned the page the protagonist would be forever changed, and there was nothing you could do about it.

When the smoke cleared, I packed my suitcase, and waited.

Mama. When it got dark out, she heated her curling iron and I knew from the smell that she was leaving. Dressed in colours, painted lips, intentional charred black around the eyes, hair curled then brushed straight. She wore this blazer with shoulder pads. I never understood why someone would want to pad their shoulders other than a football or hockey player. She always had so many things in her purse. Why did she need thirteen tubes of empty lipstick from which she pried out the residual goop with her pinky finger, pens without ink, sticks of unwrapped gum, hair scrunchies, and crumpled-up paper? I worried about her the most when she was in the bathroom. I worried about her most when the bathroom door was closed. I worried when the light under the door didn't change because I knew what the frozen light meant. I worried that she'd never come back and I would have to pack my things again. I worried that there would be a knock on the door. I worried that I'd forget books, lose hair clips, and that my bags wouldn't be big enough to hold the contents of my tiny room—the one with the one closet that housed my good four dresses and my two pairs of red shoes.

The night was dark enough to take her and not give her back. Isn't this what all kids my age worried about? Didn't they worry about the light under the door? I watched her while she rimmed her eyes with more black. She faced the mirror without blinking. She moved the pencil in slow back-and-forth strokes, her mouth a wide O that closed with a snap of her jaw when she pulled the pencil back, examining her work in that mirror. She patted her poufed hair with careful palms. She spent a lot of time in front of that mirror. I wondered why someone would need so much black. Why not green, yellow, or red? Maybe she was trying to hide the glossiness of her eyes. She seemed sad. The kind of sad where you didn't want anyone to notice, so you covered it up the best way you knew how. Maybe she was trying to shield people from the things *she* saw. But her shield didn't work on me. I saw everything.

I saw her as a young girl too. I knew her name. She was smart. She played on the playground too. She pumped her long legs on the swings and she was higher than all the other kids. She swung higher and higher and higher. She screamed, "Watch this!" and she jumped, but never landing in the way that she fell. She fell deep into the sand and she didn't get up. That's the difference between her and me. She just didn't get up.

I saw her in a dream once and I told her I loved her, but my mouth was hollow and voiceless. I mouthed the words and she faded slowly into the night, her hair haloed by the orange glow of the moon—the kind of light that slapped the sky slow—and she let the night take her. She was so beautiful. Some people said I was beautiful too. I didn't believe any of those people. They didn't see me from the inside. They wouldn't think I was beautiful if they saw.

She shoved her cigarettes in her purse and clasped it shut.

"You guys be good," she said as she turned the knob to leave.

"Where you going?"
"Out."
"Can I come?"
"Girl, please."
"Please, Mama?"
"I'll be back later."

My brother's eyes never left the TV, so if he heard her, I didn't know. He seemed more angry than sad. I watched his expression change from indifferent to fuming. I couldn't figure it out and I didn't ask him because I didn't want him to know I noticed.

Mama closed the door, and her loud footsteps up the squeaky side stairs were the only reminder that she was still there. I saw the shiny heels of her black shoes through the window I was looking out from. When the sound stopped, I quieted my breathing just in case. Just in case she changed her mind and came back to sit down next to me on the arm of the couch, pulling my hair with a brush as I wrote my name over and over at the bottom of an unlined page torn out of my best friend's notebook.

I waited for her. Late into the night. The sky was freckled with blinking yellow eyes. The moon changed position in that freckled sky the way my heart changed position in my chest. My heart couldn't get right. I couldn't let her go. I tossed and turned in my small bed. The squeaks of the mattress were more than I could bear. I wondered about the shooting feeling that moved through my neck, chest, legs, and feet when I closed my eyes. Is that what worrying did to people? I could never ask. Who would I ask? No one would understand anyway.

I lay in bed and searched the ceiling for her. The white dots played tricks on me. The ceiling seemed to move down, lowered itself until it hovered just above my eyelids. I slept with my shoes on in case she came home screaming that we had to leave. I slept in a small room with my red shoes on. I lay there in that bed. I wrote stories in my head about her taking me clothes shopping or grocery grabbing. Two hours later I lost the fight to stay awake. The red glare from my alarm clock slipped into pink haze. I closed my eyes just as my bedroom door whipped open and the light from the living room sliced me in half. She stood there in that doorway and she was beautiful. I pulled the two blankets up around my chin. One was new, warm, and patterned with dolls.

"What you doin' sleeping with those shoes on? Girl, you ain't going no-where. You hear me? You ain't going nowhere."

Dear Current Occupant: Part One

Dear Current Occupant—House with the sign in the window

Handwritten in red felt pen, a "For Rent" sign duct-taped in a window of a basement suite we used to live in. Beside it—a house, vacant, but always evidence of an occupant: garbage cans full at the curb, recycling box stacked with flattened, lidless tin cans and unrinsed milk jugs. Broken glass hung on the front porch—like family. Through an open window, I saw a girl. She was quiet. Thin. I lowered my face just below the white-paint-peeled frame. Closer. Her black hair bundled in a tight bun on her head. Her long neck seeming to struggle under the weight. She sat there on a twin mattress on the floor. She was still except for the steady back and forth of her index finger that picked at her dry knees. I watched her and I wanted to ask her questions. Were there days spent lying on this mattress and praying?

I walked over to the door, and there was a hole where a knob should have been. I pushed slightly and the squeak announced my presence. The hallway in front of me was long, narrow, wallpapered in yellow and hurt. I ran my hands along the seams and stopped in front of her open door. The doorway framed my body like a painting I once saw. She turned and looked at me funny. She squinted like she knew me. She squinted like she saw me. She said my name under her breath as if it were her own. I sat down beside her on her perfectly made bed. She lowered her knees, rolled onto her belly, put her chin in her palms, and smiled at me. But her eyes spoke of home. A house far from here. How do I bring you back home?

On a floating wall shelf above her head, a thin blanket, folded, and patterned with pink-haired dolls. I reached up and pulled it down, watched as the folds released in slow motion. With the worn patterned blanket around her pointy shoulders, I kissed her on the forehead. She laid her heavy head on a stained pillow with a sigh as her neck finally found relief.

She slept slow and long as her breath pulled and released the curtains in a back-and-forth wave, as if grazing a shoreline over and over.

I got up and walked over to her closet. Two pairs of red shoes were lined against the wood-panelled wall, four dresses hung from wire hangers in this small closet that wasn't hers—she'd never wear those dresses. I closed the door behind me. I bet she'll never find her mother.

Dear Current Occupant—Origami house with the handmade roof

I ran my hands up and down the stucco. It scratched my palms raw. The shingled roof like black patches of chocolate, a fairy-tale house, a gingerbread house. The air—it got so heavy at times. Good days held on tight to bad days. But the closer we got to the day when the money came, the heavier the smoke. Burnt like metal spoons, the black undersides acted as witnesses. The pools filled behind my eyes. As she worked, I watched the corners of her mouth turn down.

Time elapsed backwards. Window breeze blitzed her hair slow. The way she spoke into that phone, wrapped the cord around her finger, asked for things without blinking. Unfolded the corners first. Swam in white. She whispered, "There's always been treasures at the end."

I was six. I learned that being a woman meant drinking deep-red liquid from green, slim-necked bottles held in shaky palms. Nails painted a cool chipped blue and burgundy lipstick rimmed the edges of fast-emptied glasses that made a clanking noise against stained teeth—led to late nights spent with shrieking laughter. And women—deep in the red. Peered through the cracked bedroom door. Lowered eyelids and mini-envelopes so intricately folded, and each flap lifted in slow motion. Sprinkled the white powder onto the glass coffee table. I knew how to be a woman. My red shoes. Dusted in white.

Dear Current Occupant—Duplex near Fraser Street with the picture books in the closet

Believe in fairy tales? A nasty habit, mixed with dreaming out loud, or feeling high. I wanted someone to take me away from there. I looked out of a small oval window and compared the city's skyline to the ones I'd seen in pictures or a painting I once saw. The breeze came in softer, softest. I needed to know the colour of shattered people. Outside my small window, painted clouds hid the sounds of the breaking. People were broken. Like me. Like homes. What was it that made a house a home?

Our kitchen was big, and the floor held my feet hostage. Small brown and grey tiles. I tried counting them one Saturday when the cable was out. Three hundred and eighty-one. They sat within each other—layered. Kitchen table in the corner, not on display. Never had plates as visitors. No cracked cups or chipped mugs.

The closet in my room was mine. My books lined the shelves and spanned six feet. Tales of happily-ever-afters and pictures of big bright houses. Houses.

Mama said, "Gather what you can, we're leaving."

I didn't question her. I wanted her to be okay.

The day we left, my books didn't fit in my pocket.

Dear Current Occupant—Letter to Santa

Don't ever leave your favourite book unattended. Imagine someone else turning its pages, creasing its spine, running their fingers up and down the words you've already memorized. There's something you need to know about winter.

You'll spend your first ten years wishing for snow. You'll peer out from frosted windows waiting for the sky to offer cold flakes. Your eyes will remain frozen in a way no one can explain. You'll sit alone in your room writing letters about what you didn't want. But—what is it you need? Make a list of the thing you don't want. Clear the space. Make room.

Leave them your rings, your bike, your hair clips, your headbands, your books, your first bra, your handwritten notes, your favourite shirt, your old teddy bear, your fear, your sadness, your last-calls, your please-helps, your no-one-will-love-yous, your you-don't-fit-heres, your no-not-yous, your not-really-what-we-wanteds. Just go ahead and leave them the rings, the coins in between the couch cushions, the one morning cartoon, the last slice of bread, the mismatched socks, the missing spoons, the expired milk,

just make sure you leave them my goddamn rings.

Dear Current Occupant—House with the green door on East 12th Avenue

My uncle bought me a diamond ring. It was layered. It moved. I wore it on my middle finger. Left hand. I'd swing the layered pieces with my thumb. I felt beautiful. I still find it hard to say—I felt worthy of its shine. In this house I had this ring and I was queen. I was unstoppable. I wore this crown on my finger to school. I protected my ring from paint.

In school, brown was one of the colours I refused. I wouldn't paint.

I don't miss this house. She'd open the curtains just to remove all traces of the fire. I bet he—that man Mama chose—did it on purpose, that fire. A green velvet chair next to a mattress on the floor. A cigarette lit with tired hands falls much easier from fingers. Wanted us kids gone. Wanted Mama all to himself. Turned the TV louder. Sleepless nights caused the words to come to me in droves; hung from chandeliers that swayed in the breeze from an open window and echoed off fluttering eyelids—I dreamt of a house with a green door, but I won't paint. The empty spot on the wall above the couch covered in red. I tangled my voice within the strokes of a brush.

I don't paint. I don't miss this house.

I had my own comfort. For Christmas, my uncle bought me this ring. This glorious layered ring. It was full of untouched diamonds. These diamonds hung perfectly on my finger. I had layered diamonds. That no man could take.

Dear Current Occupant—Basement suite on Earles Street

The walls housed family photos hung crookedly with old tape from the Christmas box. The ash of the carpet. The room my brother and I shared. The couch Mama slept on. The nail that stuck out from the porch and sliced my ankle wide open. Mama's one good boyfriend who made me laugh with the way he walked.

I tried to keep Mama safe. She had demons. On the day the money came, I pictured those demons grabbing a hold of her, wrapping vine-like arms around her throat, squeezing until she gave in. She was strong, but Lord knows, it was stronger. Imagine what it sounded like or how loud it was. I faked being sick in the schoolyard at recess and lunch. Keeled over in pain on the metal swings, letting the chains slap my face as I hit the ground. My teacher ran over. He rubbed his hand down my back. Felt the curve of my spine, the bones. Then my stomach. "Tell me what the pain feels like," he asked as he squeezed me.

I wondered what it was that made me strong. Why did I worry? Why did I always need to make sure everyone else was still breathing? It can't always be kisses and hugs.

"I feel so sick."

"Let me get you home. What's your address? Is your mother home?"

"I live behind a tree with flowers covered in pink."

He drove me home. I checked on her. Got it down to a science. Practised in front of the bathroom mirror—held my breath, watched the colour of my skin change, furrowed my brows and wrapped my arms around my waist for emphasis. Came home and wrote poems about death. Wrote poems about being saved. Wrote poems about men, teachers. Wrote poems where I was somewhere else and my mama loved me and told me I was beautiful. I recited them over and over like mantras or prayers. Stared at her from across the room. Hoped she heard them though I wouldn't dare say them aloud. She didn't allow feelings to be aired. She just didn't want to hear it.

"I love you."

"Nobody wants to hear that shit."

I hid notebooks, like I did something wrong. My brother didn't worry as much. If he did, I didn't know it. He got angry at times. He wanted more.

I looked at him. On his bed. His side of the room plastered in pages. His posters were cut and ripped from magazines. Men in mid-air, jaws clenched as if to say, "I have to do this," and these occupied the entire wall—these men with the jaws in pain.

"Why do you have so many of those posters?" I'd ask my brother.

He tossed his ball against the wall, speaking between the thuds. "One day I'ma be in the NBA."

"What's an NBA?"

"Sis, you need to learn!"

He threw a blue-and-yellow jersey at me. I put it on. Across the back it read "Webber."

I fell asleep with my arms folded across the fabric.

Dear Current Occupant—Apartment above the East Indian sweet shop just off 49th

The purple-striped shirt I wore when Mama finally came home after being gone for three whole days; the smell of the bathroom when the curling iron heated to 400 degrees and melted the plastic countertop; the wiry hair texture of the imitation Barbie doll I got after waiting in line for hours at the place where they gave toys to kids who otherwise wouldn't get one— I wanted a white teddy bear with the red bow neatly tied around its neck—

 I wanted to put him next to my pillow, that bear. Instead I clenched into a ball when Auntie came to take my brother for the weekend and left me behind. Was it because I was a girl? I couldn't be sure but I started to feel bad about being a girl and thought that maybe if I wasn't a girl, things would get better, easier. So I started tying my hair up tight. Big sweaters, dark colours. Tried to bend reality. Things should have gotten better.

My pillow smelled of cardamom and fennel. I buried my nose in the fabric.

"She's so quiet," they all said. "She doesn't talk." They'd always say this. Maybe no one ever asked the right questions.

I looked around the room. How much time will I have this room? I asked the voice inside my head. I loved the wood floors.

In the morning I woke to the sound of a car door slamming.

Dear Current Occupant—Palms Motel, Kingsway

The whizzing of cars, the red, orange, then green light that bled through the curtains in thirty-second intervals. There was a normalcy to this. Inside this room, the two queen beds with a dark floral pattern and a seven-inch space between them hid fourteen garbage bags full of clothes shoved directly beneath. We couldn't get mail there. I remember saying out loud, "How will we get our mail?"

A strange thing to be concerned about, mail.

Mama was always in the bathroom. Every few minutes I watched the light change and deepen between the door and the linoleum, waited for shadow and movement.

The buzzing of the neighbours' TV didn't affect me doing my homework. My brother lay on the bed, tossed his basketball against the wall over and over, the expected rhythm of this a relaxing piece of normal. Quiet would be suspicious. Silence caused more questions. I wrote my name on my English paper, erased the C at the beginning and the E at the end. Helen. I stared at it for a full minute. I could be someone else with this pencil, its end yielding the power to erase. To start over.

Dear Current Occupant—House we all shared on Forgotten Street

Ten people in a three-bedroom upper suite. Vancouver Special. The walls covered in tiny fingerprints. Bugs in the bed, crumbs on the stove, broken Transformers and Lego pieces, and Cheerios and dirty mismatched socks scattered on the beige carpet. I kept my small treasures under my pillow. We were visitors there. On a small couch with sixty dollars under my pillow, I slept. Never saw the shadow of a body get closer. Never saw her walk away when she had second thoughts at the last minute. Never felt the hand that reached underneath my head. Never felt the tingling of fingers accidentally grazing the small hairs behind my ear. Never heard the rustling of bills between sly fingers. Never woke up to see the sadness in the whites of eyes or the remorse as she placed the money in her pocket. Never saw her turn back and double-check that I was still asleep and maybe even feel sorry enough to offer me a short, warm kiss on my cheek or tuck the edge of the blue blanket into the crook of my sweaty neck. I didn't wake up in time.

Dear Current Occupant—Two-toned red-and-white brick house on 41st behind the church

I wake to the sound of the church bell, the sweetness of the crab-tree smell in the air—the one in the back on the tiny hill, and the wailing voices from inside. Those voices. My brother's best friend and his sister lived across the street from the church. They were not allowed to cross over. I never understood why. Our house, a basement. In the yard, a shed. It was locked. I wondered what was in there. I was five. Mama wanted me to walk to school by myself. I wouldn't. The sound of the church bells scared me. The unfamiliar smell of the flowers falling from the branches of the trees in the alley made me sick.

After school I sat on a metal fence, thinking of the church, the bells, and our friends who couldn't cross over. Two sisters looked for me, pushed me, laughed.

I went home.

"What's wrong?" Mama asked.

"There's these two girls, they're in grade seven, they beat me up every day."

Mama said nothing. Butted out her cigarette into the almost-full glass ashtray. She stood up, pushed her chair in. The bang of the metal against the table made me jump.

She left the house and slammed the door behind her. I sat at the kitchen table for twenty minutes. Looked at the trees I hated so much.

Mama came back. "They won't bother you no more, ya hear?"

I nodded.

After school most days I'd sit on a metal fence, thinking of the church, the bells, and our friend who wouldn't cross over. Two sisters walked past me. Lowered their heads, their hands deep in their pockets.

Witness Statements

I didn't have a father. The one time I went to his house, I knew I didn't fit there. The carpet hugged the space between my toes. So many stairs. Down, up, down again. Never-ending stairs. His son and daughter had their own rooms. His wife had short hair. The kitchen table held large dishes of corn, potatoes, tandoori-style chicken. I was drawn to serving spoons, their largeness, what they could hold—what they could dump out. One spoon had a plastic black handle. The other, metal. I wanted those spoons.

I sat across from my father. My half-brother to my left, my half-sister to my right. I was in the middle even though I was on the outside, and older. They were more interested in each other than in me. Bobbed and weaved around me while they laughed and whispered in each other's ears. They knew he didn't want me there. I watched my father eat. I was young. His mouth and nose matched mine. He held his fork with a firm grip. His knuckles white. We reached for the pepper at the same time. I looked down at my plate until he was done. Pepper was my favourite. His too. Both our plates covered in black specks.

No one asked me about school, or friends, or writing, or home. No one asked me about home. I didn't know how I got there, to this house built not for me. I wanted to take the bus, sit at the back, open the window, and let the wind bury my face in my hands, never go back there.

Instead, I slept in the basement on an L-shaped couch. Surrounded by boxes, old exercise equipment, and items to be discarded labelled "Barely yard sale worthy." My eyes held the ceiling up all night.

"One day I will teach you to drive," he said.

Two and a half decades pass.

I never got my licence but I have two large serving spoons in my kitchen drawer.

Pack your things. A phrase that scared me more than any other. When I got home from school I opened my dresser drawers and I prepared to pack my things. I never once owned a desk.

Pack your things.
Pack your things.
Pack your things.

In the cab ride there, I dreamt:

In the next apartment, I will be older. I'll have learned some things. The milk won't expire, the rent will be paid, no one will find us. And me? I'll have a pet, a dog.

apartment 301 near the low track

When your house catches fire, I'll free the dogs.
I'll wrap your vases in paper and stop
fingers from shakin'. Look you in the eye.
I'll consider pink sheepskin, I sleep in
the holes of my pockets, my hands dug deep.
No coins, no bills, but ain't no poor one here.
I still got jewels in throat—embedded,
planted well behind the voice, the word box,
and still the birds flock round me, as they should.
We got things to get done, they'd say. I'll stand
there—solid. My face red, hot, wet, hungry.
Feed the hand, or the hand that feeds us all.
It don't matter where you grow it, we'll eat.
Black stones in a white fire, the flame—washed out.

white house where some family lived upstairs,

Fear the caging of birds. Strangled and brown.
Moving here was like crossing a river,
debriefings, scaling back. Clay pots clogged,
awkward like an ingrown hair, browning down
in the sun. Staring at walls draws a crowd,
like a hardened nipple, a tear-streaked thigh.
No more packing things in paper, she says.
She throws screams while running and looking back.
Nothing will blossom in this heat, heavy
holding, hurry and hurt; all these h words,
but never heal. Never healing, at all.
Finding a spot to sit still, fill my cup,
empty it out, pouring steam down drains—I
am the one left clawing at the cage door.

most holidays

Ask yourself where the feathers pierce the skin.
Flesh and fingers poking in brown, those pools
of speaking. Her laughter turned down, pushed past
the uncles claiming their plate's short a stack
of black and baked—that middle-aged spread, that story.
The parents have bizarre thoughts of the sons
saved by the wolf, an axe, and a ruby ring.
Used to this sort of thing by now, they sing.
A kind of coffin, a celebration
sliced thin, like wings, dark meat, and beginnings.
A host placed in a box, before the crowd.
A candle and a scent washed out.
Lie on the floor and wait for the questions.
When no one asks, you wash your hands and leave.

like a lion in the trees

Rooftops, sightlines, and flies stuck between screens
dead orchids buried in textured glossy
white vases black picture frames that can turn
the other cheek I've heard moving art die
a slow shift pull me into a body
made from hands I've seen red bleed from beige crawl
from spaces made from sand there's a limit
to this hiding no pages will fall from
this book rip the errors from your brain
the guilt will kill you—for me you'll wait years
like a lion in the trees

of the last house I remember,

It is so ordered.

It was always about going back home.
No hands around your throat, heat of the night.
Backyards silent. Let these children play. Now,
you may never know how the pull between
two sets of lips feels, or the warm air stuck
in between the two. This may be so. Yes,
it was only about going back. Back
to the bricks that line the path to the house
with the one yellow light lit to guide them
inside, to the knee socks and high-waisted
pants—to the simple things. Not left alone.
A clothesline hung from thick rope is the only
piece of sweet silence, swingin' north to south,
between two poles planted deep in the dirt.

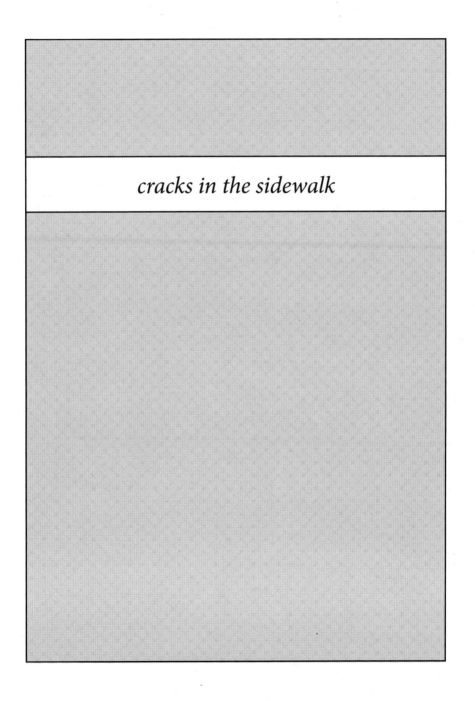

cracks in the sidewalk

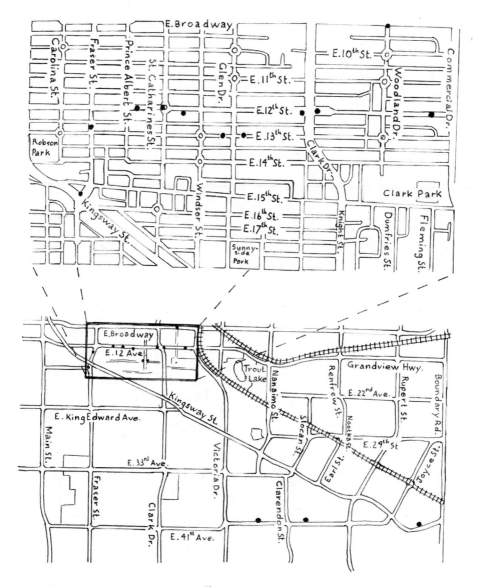

Walking tour, a map

Broadway and Commercial

41st Avenue between Victoria and Elliott, back

Clark Drive 2

Clark Drive 3

East 12th Avenue (off Commercial)

41st Avenue between Wales and Clarendon

East 12th between Windsor and Fraser, back alley

East 12th between Windsor and Fraser, back alley

Clark Drive traffic

East 12th between Windsor and Fraser, front door

East 13th Avenue, attic

East 13th Avenue, front

East 41st between Victoria and Elliott

Broadway and Commercial, back

East 41st between Victoria and Elliott, roof

Fraser and 13th

Kingsway and Fraser

Kingsway Hotel

Kingsway Hotel, side view

View from front window of East 12th

Gate, white house

Clark Drive intersection

Mailboxes

Dear Current Occupant: Part Two

Dear Current Occupant—She's at the recovery house for the third time,

A few things you need to know about her, now that you've got her. It's her third time here. She does things. She does things when the sleep won't come, like stacking towels, words, and lines.

Predictions:

She'll take the garbage out in the misty black of night. She'll roll her pant legs up and cinch the belt around her robe real tight. It's a bit of a walk, like a runway, and she'll be paradin' down to dumpsters. She won't mind if there are eyes all over. She'll pin her hair up, and it'll be the only time she seems confident.

She'll tell you stories. Gain your trust. You'll fall for it because you have no choice. You'll offer her a seat next to you. "Don't mind if I do," she'll say. She'll sweep strands upward. Pile them high. Pin them still. Listen. With the sharp edge of her tongue, she'll soften as hands send fire up the back of her own neck.

They'll tell you she's crazy. They'll tell you it's cold out these days and ain't no way her thin skin would survive it. In the dark. She does things when the sleep won't come, like stacking towels, words, and lines.

Dear Current Occupant—Apartment on Clark Drive above the convenience store,

There was a girl next door. Gave her my old backpack with the yellow and green lightning bolts on it. She knocked on our door often. She asked for things, she was curious about me, my room, our house. She peered over my shoulder when I opened the door. I asked her if she was trying to escape. She looked down at her feet just like I used to.

It was always silent across the hall.

She'd knock three times a day to borrow things: sugar, milk, flour, eggs.

"Are you baking over there?"

"No," she said.

She asked for things we didn't have.

She stood there and twisted her hair into thin braids.

She never stepped foot inside. Wouldn't cross the door frame.

She looked down at her feet just like I used to.

Dear Current Occupant—For Uncle Eugene

Fried chicken, steamed broccoli, mashed potatoes. I remember how much I looked forward to this. Staying over. You stood in the doorway of my grade five classroom. You brought me foot-long sandwiches from Subway, made sure I had money, made sure I was okay. You bought me a black-and-yellow bike. You bought me a diamond ring for my birthday. Told me I was special and I believed it. Made me and all the cousins laugh at Christmas dinners—dancing, smiling, blasting "Too Short" on your ghetto blaster, BBQs at Kits Beach. "The Knights," your sign said, bolted to a tree in the shade. You made a home for me when there wasn't one. You were all about family. You told me, "Get your grade twelve, that's all you gotta do is get your grade twelve." Your last words to me were "You make a good mac 'n' cheese." I see you when I close my eyes, and I see you when I think about what a dad should be. Thanks, Unc.

Dear Current Occupant—Owl House Women and Children's Shelter,

Sheets of metal wrapped the wood like shawls on shoulders. One door and thousands of windows. Thousands of windows, curtains drawn, no light haloed, no bodies moved, no one to put on the morning coffee and the day-starting eggs. There was no cooking here. We weren't in charge of our daily meals. Ate from plates placed in front of us, already filled, with things I wouldn't eat. At night, I'd look through barred windows, and in the distance, the only light was released from the work shed, removing its shield of dark and bouncing back to this house with the thousands of windows. Then the colours came. That slow orange light with dusty pink—some would call it rose, or maybe the "colour that comes before the bleeding starts." It took its time. The metal probably got hot when the slow light spoke and singed the fingertips of those who got too curious. I felt safe. They did our laundry on Wednesdays. Felt so secure seeing shirts and pants with endless folds and creases, one on top of the other. Mama fought and argued, got them to break the rules so I could have the toast I liked. It was all I would eat. I was too skinny, they'd say. I would take my time doing my hair, everyone said I had beautiful hair. I loved the way Mama would stick up for me, when the other families' children threw their stones. Funny, they never broke a single window.

Dear Current Occupant—The room in the attic of the oldest place we've stayed

We ate the same meal at separate tables. Next to her half-full plate. With a pink hooded sweater, I covered the skin given to me by my mother. I looked over at her, imagined her to be incredibly cultured, with white pearls around her neck. She'd have a husband. Suit and tie. He'd be tired after work. He'd light a cigarette and tell her about his day. He'd smooth out the wrinkles in her dress. He'd kiss her on the back of her neck. He'd bring her flowers "just because" and she'd feel on top of the world. He'd bring her coffee, black, and she'd fall in love all over again. He'd tuck her hair behind her ear—

but remember: a young man will lay his hands on her. He will always lay his hands on her. His hands. And tell her she's beneath him. Then—claim love. There'd be shade in the garden most days. Always a spot behind the wooden bench and large oak. A space to hide many things.

Dear Current Occupant—Pink building, Broadway and 12th,

My neighbour was like a girl falling and stuck in the scent of clove and heavy spice. One narrow pink hallway separated our apartments. Her image faded as air between two things, two people, two voices, widened. Every day she asked for things. Things I wouldn't do. She wanted help. She wanted to get better. She said strange things. She knocked on my door when Mama wasn't home. She said things like "Don't forget to take out the trash cans on Tuesday" and "Let the dog out." "You should tell your mother to put apples in your lunch bag." "Your mother has died, but let the dog out." None of it was true. We didn't have a dog. My mother was alive. I always ate apples.

I watched her lock the door behind her. I watched her come home at night, her face tired and her eyes thick-rimmed and black-smudged. Her hair a dry golden halo. I listened for voices. I wondered what she did inside those walls, even though I already knew. But this was her and she was always falling. She reminded me of bread baking. A slow rise, a slight leavening, thick and solid—flavour resting, hovering in the air just above the chin—then sinking. The recipe wasn't right. Whispered those strange things again. Sometimes so soft and smooth-like and then sharp like she hid broken saw blades between her teeth. She changed from opaque to transparent. Like an egg cooking in reverse. Cracking it into a hot skillet, and watching that translucence solidify and change to pure white. Saw her less. Felt her less. Couldn't hear her. I waited in the space just below the tallest of cement buildings closest to this house. Looked up and hoped she would come—

but praying to God that she didn't.

Dear Current Occupant—House with the attic apartment where kittens disappear,

Duct tape comes in handy when you're nine or ten years old, and you share a room with your fourteen-year-old brother. I remember drawing a line down the room: "Stay on your side."

Mama came home one night smiling, scenting the air with her breath.

She brought home five kittens. One was a soft white. I put them in the bathtub. I loved them. Stayed up all night staring at them and playing with them. Naming them. Came home from school the next day. They were gone. "Mama! Where are my kittens?"

A beat.

"I gave them back. Now go clean your room, and pick up all that damn duct tape."

Dear Current Occupant—Neighbour, this is for your daughter,

When all else fails, build a fort. Take all the blankets, sheets, pillowcases, scarves, and curtains and drape them over kitchen chairs, desks, and tables. Take books—the heavy ones—and place them on the corners of the sheets. You need to be strategic about the placement. Always strategic. Consider the centre—you don't want the middle caving down. You want to be able to stand up if you need to. You want to be able to hide if you need to. You want to be able to block out the light and the sound of your breathing if you need to. This isn't the first time I've built my own place. When all else fails, build a fort.

Dear Current Occupant—One-room apartment above the grocery store,

I wondered if the fruit felt too. Everyone picking and choosing and touching and smelling and pressing—looking for the best. Living here, I discovered the truth about how to eat a papaya.

1.

Look for skin turning from green to yellow.

Parts may look bruised. Press your thumb into the flesh.

2.

One to three days on your counter will do.

Scoop out and discard the black seeds from the centre.

3.

Run your knife downward along the skin. Slowly.

The flesh will be soft.

4.

You may not eat the skin.

Dear Current Occupant—Third-floor corner unit apartment, East Broadway,

There were bundles of cash hidden under my twin mattress. I was sixteen. He knocked on my door every couple of hours, handed me bills, wads of cash, red, green, brown—folded. "Hide this," he said. I was scared, I was in love, I was young. I wanted to be wanted and so I did as I was told. He trusted me. But I could run. I could take this money and start a life somewhere else and no one would look for me. Not in the space between the stairs, the basement of my school, the café where I did my homework—not anywhere. I could run.

I went to the mall. A man approached. "You're beautiful and you could model. Come with me."

The weeks I spent in Edmonton…these men…the things they tried to do…

A phone call home from a pay phone: "Mom, help me. Bring me back home."

Dear Current Occupant—House where I accidentally dyed my hair blond,

White. White blond. Mama laughed, her mouth held a position I'd never seen in all my sixteen and a half years—she was happy. I dyed my hair in the small bathroom of a basement suite we once lived in. I had a room here. I loved this room. I missed this room. There were stairs in the living room that led to family. "Auntie Sandra Buddy!" my cousin would yell, her toddler face squished between the bottom of the door and the stairs. "I come down?" she requested. The happiness here cradled against a moment— deserved. With this I frame an eight-by-ten photo of that smile, that position her mouth held.

Dear Current Occupant—Of every yard I didn't have

The part of the soil beneath, held together

by the roots, or a piece of thin material.

Many varieties grown in one location

to best suit the consumer's use, preference, appearance.

It undergoes fertilization, frequent watering, frequent mowing,

and subsequent vacuuming to remove the clippings.

It doesn't need to be washed clean of soil down to the bare roots,

and time to export is shortened. It has been developed

by a method of cultivating. Sprigging where recently harvested,
    cut into slender

rows and rows and   rows and rows   replanted   in the field.

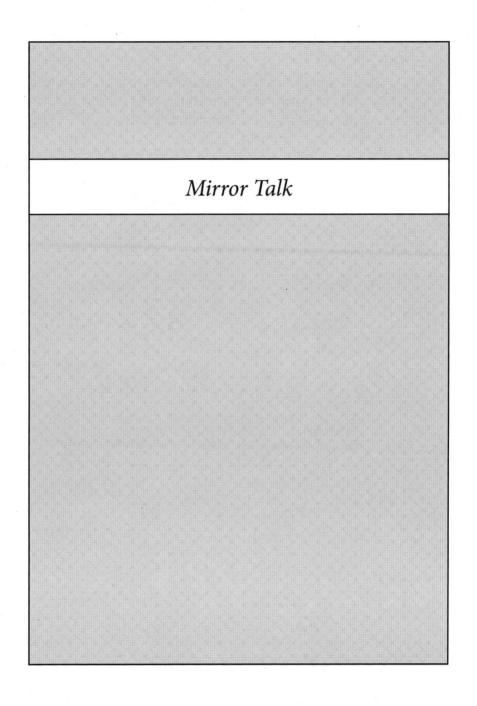

Mirror Talk

let your hair down. It was like a song she wrote just for me. She told me that a woman with long hair had to take care of it. Brush it. Pull it. Lay it flat. She said that I had good hair and that I had to let everyone see. I had to let everyone touch it and run their hands through it. I had to let everyone touch it as if it weren't even mine and it didn't belong to me. I had to let everyone see what they didn't have and couldn't have. I couldn't hide with a tightly pulled bun. No one would think I was beautiful. She said this. Let your hair down. It was like a song she wrote just for me. Brush it, pull it, lay it flat.

the eyes have it. I tried to line my eyes with charred black like her. I poked the insides, turning the whites grey and red. I stood on a wobbly stool so my face met the mirror. There's a sadness behind your eyes, she said. Don't let them see. She showed me how to hold the pencil just right. You need the right grip, she said. Just go back and forth and back and forth. See?

But I didn't see. I didn't think I ever would.

these hands *will always do the work of the empty.* This was the line I wrote down in my very first notebook. I ran my fingers over the indents the pen left on the page. Traced my fingers over my words.

I wonder what I meant by this. Was it for my mother? How did she feel about her hands? Their shape, size, the lines—did she even look at them? I never saw her paint her nails in any colour.

these lips taste water and should hold the colour when wet. Paint between the lines. Leave your mark behind if you need to. Colour on collars, prints on glasses, let them know you were there. No two lips are the same. If you want to move on with your life, listen to your dreams. Move your mouth in such a way, make them listen. Watch their eyes follow your lips when you puff on a cigarette, wrap around the edge of a glass, or touch skin.

She lined her lips in red.

I watched her as I stood in the door and wondered why she said those things to herself. But red. This was a colour I liked.

Notices of Termination

the occupants of these suites must adhere to the following rules:

Do not

cause damage to the walls, doors, or windows.

Do not

smoke inside. There will be a charge.

Do not

allow others to reside with you. There will be a charge.

Do not

fail to pay your rent on time. There will be a charge.

Do not

have pets of any kind. This means cats, dogs, and anything that crawls.

Do not

make noise past 11:00 p.m. Consider your neighbours.

Do not

think for a minute that we are not watching you.

Never leave your children alone. We will NOT be held responsible.

damage noted

Small dogs lowered their tails when you walked by. I don't remember having a pet, or anything that crawled. I had two hamsters that bit each other to death and I remember thinking, lucky you. No dogs allowed meant don't let anyone see it walking the halls. I imagined petting the fur. Three girls on the second floor had birds. I watched from my window as the girls poked them with sharpened pencils, and I used to think about the feathers they were losing. I was so glad to be moving. Mama wouldn't bother looking for boxes. No delicates to be packed or to be wrapped—I was careful with my books. No holes in the walls for bookshelves. No graffiti in the lobby in colours that offend. Your rules were endless. But you had no control over the way I made my bed. Thick-quilted patchwork squares tousled just because. Things under my pillow easy for the taking, a safe with no key. One book I've never read: "technicolored complaints aimed at my head."[1]

The man upstairs would stare at me the mornings I went to school.

You had no rule for this. My backpack carrying different paths no one could follow. Close behind, linger—jump out wide-armed from bushes. I never carried myself. I used to wish that man would die from overdose, mash up upon my door like mosquitoes. Vancouver. Civilization, people, government. All the city's children are safe? Peeled back the scalps of white Barbie dolls half-eaten, chewed, spat out on the floor. Worrying about the stained carpet still, Mama cleans. She cannot whiten the stain, no matter how hard she tries. Sweep like empty ladles through the lobby of my eyes.[2]

---

1 Line from "Moving Out or the End of Cooperative Living" by Audre Lorde.

2 Line from "Moving Out or the End of Cooperative Living" by Audre Lorde.

I broke the rules on purpose

In the basement, all the secrets slept and woke on time every single night. Many people stayed for free on sundecks, balconies, and stairs. I saw them in the fetal, a position we all once held. I asked the people who boarded with us if they had problems too. There were conversations on the couch.

"What do you want to be when you grow up?"

"A chef."

"Oh yeah, are you a good cook?"

"I'm picky, my mom says."

This man put his hand on my leg. He left it there for a while.

I stood up.

I crept out of my mother's house. With nothing in my pockets.

someone slashed the tops off coconuts so we could drink the milk

My shoulder bones inverted when they saw Mama sleeping next to blood-spotted walls and counters, cigarette-burnt carpets. Standing there in a house not ours, I wondered how words scarred her cheek, how the basement water rose above the head just enough to stop her breathing chest from expanding—but didn't. When she woke she gathered her things, her winter, her warmth, and her liquids.

Present time. In the water you wade.

Everything on the shore was half-buried beneath the green-and-blue seas. Silk settled on shoulders—her hunched back mirrored the stacks of mountains. This weight, these stacks, trembled under wet lips, thirsty lips. There was a promise made about where we would go. We were supposed to run away from here. We got lost. She got lost. But it's quiet now looking back in time as yellow umbrellas flicker like cracks in the brain. How else would I have known these particular facts that bashed me against the rocks? Still places to go and unpaid bills piling on hillsides. As any second eviscerates a breath.[3]

---

3 A line from Dionne Brand's "Thirsty."

Miss Parker

i

Bring me back home, she says, lifting silver
teacups, saucers—the pot bone-dry. Fingers
rubbing chicken skin injecting pickle juice.
She smiles thinkin' this is how we do it
down here. No walls, no roof,
knees worn to their fossil resin.
Porch won't give in under her weight.
Floorboards shifting, holding,
begging. This is home.
Dresses from newspaper
patterns crafted by hand.
Never tear down any part
left standing, the wind picks who
stays planted. No cotton here in this field.

ii

Stays planted. No cotton here in this field.
Refusing to lay her head down.
Butterfly windows kiss when closed.
Can't hang them any kind of way, you hear?
Dig where roots lay, sleep deep in the narrow,
napes of necks and small white hairs fall back
and stand up—
this is close-quarter breathing.
The rise and fall worth more.
A needing. Eating on plates, with brothers.
A daughter's come back to fill
rooms heavy with voices,
big-city breathing, under
the wood floors, there's still water trickling
into the cold of night air, it rises.

iii

Into the cold of night air it rises
like full white bellies and greased-up fingers.
Tops of washed-up houses sweep by
your feet, can't walk
on no more nails. Haystacks
on the backs of trucks, tires stuck in mud, stop
the heat from leaking—it gets cold in there
most nights. Rooms, colour schemes,
holy water. Anything of value—
gone.
A place to stay. Sweet-potato-
pumpkin pie. Actions speak
like long, curly black hair dragged down the steps.
She took a trip backwards, calling her name.

iv

She took a trip backwards, calling her name.
Embedded in marble
    —a sprawling swamp.
Her name was removed and replaced. Pink stacks
falling apart. Stretched mouths
bite
outside, inside, come up slow. The sun,
like frying turkey, it sizzles,
burns—
Get back. Leather-wrapped hands,
the roots, the family:
paint them.
Play the music. Beside the fence. Press pause.
Lord, blessed with abundance, flatlined and back.

v

Lord, blessed with abundance, flatlined and back,
a visit in November comes early.
Homesick, hungry, stuck in the flux,
she trembles. Never happened,
this thing, held her arms behind her head.
Waiting to raise
the covers atop her face.
Still breathing.
Lost in the black heap, he speaks
in the confines of the trailer,
she puts her shoes on.
She knows, somebody heard her,
part of them is gone.
At dawn, another house rolls down the street.

vi

At dawn, another house rolls down the street
made of ashes, of summer, bolts of spring leaves,
all seasons meeting for tea, it's pleasant
in a world tucked under,
flipped over—a spot to rest her knees.
Yellow trims and frames corners of eyes—
closed shut. Hush of the hinges
folding, hollow echoes
whip the air. Fair-skin mistakes float past, knowing
the water in the well's run dry. Tonight,
we'll call for masses. Fill the streets
lined deep with bodies,
bordered with lilies.
Tonight, she'll speak in two-tone. Silver   gold.

vii

Tonight, she'll speak in two-tone. Silver, gold.
Lay claim to the structure
of bone. Sons, talkin' old times
in the kitchen, no water came,
nothing ripped from walls
    left floating,
knees not bending, no ache,
no jewels thieved, no coins
clenched in the fists of uniformed men, no
pleading on rooftops for rescue for days,
left counting bodies, family
lost, limbs hover from high white ceilings.

Miss Parker. Miss Parker? Miss, are you there?
Bring me back home, she says. Lifting. Silver.

Lay your head on my pillow. Wake up next to me. Put your arm right in the curve between my hips and ribs. Pull me closer. Wrap your legs around mine, they aren't heavy. The weight of them keeps me still. I whisper, you're my hero and you saved me. You pull the blanket up around my chin and tell me you love me with all your heart. You turn your body around and I follow with mine. I follow the angular curve of your ear with the tip of my finger. The light from our window (*our* window) bleeds the light in, warm and permanent.

In this moment, I find love. Permanent, like the pages of books. He turns the pages loud, and slow. He turns the pages like this on purpose and it sounds like the loud screech of a crow's claws sliding down a wall of freshly rained-on metal—the kind of sound that makes you want to cover your ears and slap someone all at the same time. He sits there reading *All the Light We Cannot See* while mouthing along to the words. His upper lip moving much slower than the bottom, he smiles at certain parts, clears his throat at others. Occasionally, he will stop to bite a piece of hanging skin by his nail, say "hmmm," then glance out the window and take a monstrous sip out of his giant mug of overcreamed coffee. He returns to his book, furrows his brows as if he doesn't know what the words on the page are trying to tell him, but really, he's probably just trying to look intense. Or maybe it's just a really good book. But what can be said about reading a book?

There's so much more to be seen that no one notices, but I notice. I notice the steady but slow rocking back and forth and the way he holds the spine of the book in his hands like one would cradle the neck of a newborn baby, and I wonder just then what he's thinking. I realize how beautiful he is and how the whiteness of his skin looks so soft from here and how I wish I was the spine of that book that holds together all the pages that make him mouth along to the words.

He tells me I need to know some things. He tells me about all the light he does not see, and I tell him about the light under the doors. He tells me I don't have to watch for the shifting light anymore. The shadows are gone. He tells me there is more than this. He tells me I am beautiful, and for the first time, I believe it.

epilogue

mama, you need to know some things. I did not become a mother in that house. That house. Its openings consisted of three small windows and holes in the roof. There was no door to leave from. How did we get there? Outside, the branches of a coconut tree sealed the doom of us children. The rusted white mailbox hung loosely from a nail. Our nightmares were lined in the leaves' shadows. We thought there was nothing more than this, this house. But I knew there was something more than this.

So at night I slept; the dawn came; I went to work; the dusk fell. At work I roasted coffee beans, pounded them into a coarse powder. I watched as my taste buds were flung into the atmosphere in slow motion like small eruptions inside my heart. How could I become a mother? How could I become a mother when I have seen the way the unmoving light under a door could scrape a young girl from the inside out?

I worked three jobs. I went to school. I wrote stories. I did everything I was told I couldn't.

When I moved out, you made sure I couldn't buy clothes. You told me I would waste away from hunger, I wouldn't make it on my own. I would fade into a pile of ash at your feet. I ate sandwiches Monday to Friday, bagels on the weekends. You didn't want me to leave you, and your reasons made my throat clench.

"I need that money," you said.

"But, Mama, I have to go, I can't stay here forever."

"Pfft, you think you grown, don't you?"

"I am grown, I'm eighteen now."

I looked you in the eye. I wanted you to hug me and tell me you were proud of me. I wanted to tell you that I was born already grown and that I didn't ask for that. I wanted to tell you I loved you and wished you could say the same.

I packed up my things up in that small room. I taped the bottoms of boxes with black tape I found in the kitchen drawer. I lined the bottoms of the boxes over and over with black. I pressed my palms down firmly along the black seams I created. My books fit perfectly into those boxes. Every last one of them. I ripped the blue bedsheet disguised as curtains from the rod, and the roof shook. I pulled my posters down from those walls wall-papered in yellow and hurt. The walls dropped the three small mirrors on their own. I picked them up from the floor, wrapped them in yesterday's newspaper. I pulled back the wood-panelled doors of my small closet, and the hinges screeched my name. I had one old pair of khaki pants, and an old shirt of some kind of cotton. I kept my pants folded in the way they were creased. The iron I used reminded me of the melted plastic counter-top and singed hair.

As I packed, I dreamt of a dark house. A house in the woods. We never lived there. But in this house the wooden slats were tilted, and measured three inches across the floor. They created a pattern of shading and light. The kind of light that could fully clothe any woman. In this house we didn't have much: a kerosene lamp, white enamel basins, rusted hinges—all hud-dled on a mahogany table. The curtainless windows let the light eat the walls. There was a breeze, even when every window was closed.

In that house I dreamt about death—a lot. I dreamt that I may not have lived to see the night. I know this is difficult for you to hear, but when you don't want to think too much, say nothing and I'll hear you. When I was a girl, in my room, and you came home at night, I heard the sound of his boots on the cobblestones. He knocked at the door. I thought, I could easily cut off his head. He wore a blue shirt—the shade of blue that the sea be-came at midday. His colour-worn shoes bathed a scent no man could ever afford. Did you know that? I saw everything. I heard it all.

We were hungry most nights. You managed to bring food in the night. I was picky. I am sorry for that. It's as if I would eat nothing but fig leaves wrapped tight and placed carefully in a knapsack as heavy as cloth buckets filled with black sand. I didn't make it easy, did I?

The bathroom housed my things too. My brushes, hair clips, face cream, and toothbrush. I was always afraid of the smallness of bathrooms. I stood there in the doorway with a small taped box in my hand. In the mirror, I saw the fear on my own face in every shallow surface and crevice, but I reminded myself that I could cause my own demise with complete calm.

But I wanted to let you know some things. I never dreamt of becoming a mother. Not in that house. Not in any of those houses. I would never become a mother. I told myself that in the mirror every night: *You will never be her*. While you painted your eyes in charred black, I taught myself how to use colours. You thought I would bear children like you. You thought they'd fall and never get up. You told me this. You thought they would fall deep into the sand. But they won't. They didn't. She didn't.

I did not grow tired. I did not become a mother in this house. I did not become a woman in this house. I never once found my mother in this house, even though I looked for her nightly in the ceiling and under doors. I looked for her under the door of every single bathroom of every single house we ever lived in. I watched for the light to shift, for shadows to change. When I got scared I listened, waited, closed my eyes, fought back tears, waited again, dreamt, slept, ate, waited, and wrote stories.

So this is my story.

In this last house, I did become a woman. I listened to the voices that said I was beautiful. I did not want anyone to spend their time looking for me under bathroom doors. I did not wish that on anyone.

I may have spent all my time bedding a mattress stuffed with coconut fibre, but on my last day in that house I took every single item in that room—but I left you some things: my key looped with a small yellow ribbon on the counter underneath this letter next to a small box lined in black. Inside— four dresses and two pairs of red shoes.

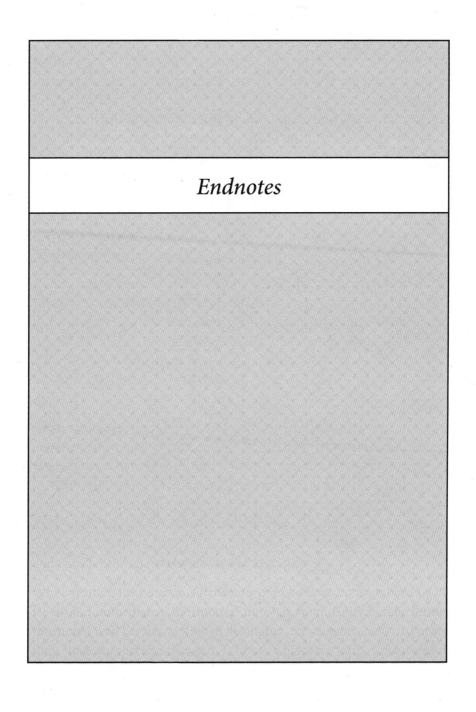

Endnotes

home. A one-syllable word like *walls*, *doors*, and *roof*. A house. Something many of us take for granted. I was drawn to the concept of home and belonging for many years, and bits and pieces of both came to life in my first book, *Braided Skin* (Mother Tongue Publishing, 2015). After this dip-my-toes-in-the-water book, I saw an unfinished thread poking out from within the pages, a story, a missing piece that needed to be told in another form, another book. *Dear Current Occupant* has been in the works for many years, even before *Braided Skin*, but it took that first book to pave the way. It took reading and listening to many other voices speak of home and lack thereof for me to start piecing together the fragments of home I have so desperately been looking for.

Genres are crossing, bending, merging, melding, and morphing into new subgenres, and this is what happened with *Dear Current Occupant*. And just like genres, the same can be said when it comes to belonging—the bending. I can never let go of the bending. The squeezing to fit into a place, a home. How many doors have to slam shut? How many windows can I look out of, trusting that the view will remain the same?

I have two photos of myself when I was young. Two. I wrote this book based on events and memories I perceived to be true at the time, and compared them to how I see things today. These stories and fragments are glimpses back in time. Sometimes when you're a kid trying to survive, the lines of reality and fantasy blur, causing you to look back years later and ask yourself, "Where do I come from, and how in the world do I find my way home?" Writing about "loss of home" by way of natural disaster, poverty, uncertainty, and troubling political times—it's all visceral and connecting, and I challenge you to convince me otherwise.

While reading Esi Edugyan's *Dreaming of Elsewhere*, I was grabbed by the lapels and immediately transported into her story. Goosebumps formed the more I read her description of belonging, unbelonging, and that unsettling shadowy space in between. Is home a place we were, a place we are, a place we want to be, or is it simply a state of being? What does home even mean? Fragments came together in various forms, and craved the folding of poetic verse. *Dear Current Occupant* is many things. It is a quilt. Each square, each patch—doin' work.

Coming from a place far from any sort of privilege, I've always made do with what I had for however long I had it. The threat of having to move at a moment's notice and leave things behind was a part of my life. I never realized there was anything different. How did others live their lives? A question that took its time.

Questions of home led to questions of family and then, finally, questions of self. I was a young girl who never realized I was a person of colour or what this meant. I rarely saw myself anywhere but the spot I was always in. No one told me to be a strong Black woman. No one told me I needed to feel comfortable in my own skin. No one told me it was okay to speak up, ask questions, change minds, be different. Esi Edugyan says, "Dreaming of elsewheres is one of the ways we struggle with the challenge of what it means to be here—by which I mean at home, in ourselves." Really, I have probably always been home, but now need to "leave in order to come back, changed. Made new."

black and female while writing.[4]

"But you don't look that Black."

I remember walking into an event where I had been asked to be a guest reader by a woman who'd "heard about" my book. We'd never met, and I was unfamiliar with the other readers, never heard of the venue, but was still interested in expanding my literary horizons. This is what emerging writers need to do, right? I introduced myself to her and she stared back at me for a good fifteen seconds before furrowing her brow and saying, "But you don't look that Black." Once again I was left feeling "less than" and not worthy of being part of the event because I didn't fit the mould of what Black should be. I didn't meet the expectations of the diversity hashtag.

My mother is an American-born Black woman. My father is an East Indian-Ugandan who was kicked out of his country for not being Black. Now I am left to question my own "Blackness" in a room full of whites whose eyes are all on me. I fumbled through my reading without ever looking up from my book.

What do comments like this mean to a mixed-race writer, woman, Canadian, artist, creator, just trying to share her stories? What if every time she woke, she saw herself as a writer sitting across the room from a Black writer?

Sometimes there is a divide, depending on where I am and whom I am with. I am split in two. The first me is comfortable in her skin, doesn't feel the need to explain her own ethnicity, while the second me comes to the table "orally armed," ready to defend myself as soon as the slightest pebble of doubt is tossed at my feet.

What does it feel like to occupy one body that is essentially your own, but as two separate people—a Black woman writer and a writer? For one, it's

---

4 Originally published as "Constantly Proving My Blackness Is Exhausting" (*Globe and Mail*, 2017).

extremely difficult to write while constantly bouncing back and forth like this. Walking into an event—a full house where you are the only non-white face—will always bring up questions: am I the physical representation of a diversity hashtag? Is my writing good? Can I read to this particular room of people?

As a woman of colour, proving my "Blackness" should never be on the list of things I need to accomplish. Like other marginalized people, I work in the mostly white world of the Canadian literary community.

I worry there is no "how to" manual to make sure everyone gets the chance to speak, and that we are offered the same opportunities. What is my responsibility to other writers who aren't white? And do I think we are being included only because an event, publication, or panel needs a writer to be "less white"? Or are we wanted because our story is important?

Will diversity and inclusivity become less of a "hot topic," so voices get muted? Will the appetite for diversity dwindle? What does it mean to be a Black writer while others question your work, your reasons for writing, and your "colour," even before you've begun to write? And who has the right to even ask?

My writing runs constant circles around these questions—who gets accepted into the literary world, who is left out, and who decides. There is a fine line between tokenism and offering up a platform for marginalized voices.

I want to be heard. But does that mean I need to scream louder than everyone else, or say something no one else is saying, and defend it to the death? While this is exhausting, through hard work, muscles form. Repeating a constant repetitive motion creates strength. It builds a confidence. And that confidence brings about trust. I'm learning we can't always question why we are being included or why we are not.

Of course, I still question what it will take before writers like myself stop seeing themselves in double? And at what point will I walk into a room full of writers, readers, panelists, and speakers without feeling like the diversity hashtag? I don't think anyone should have all the answers, but these questions will always be shouting in my mind until we do.

I just hope my stories will shout louder.

I wrote this book for many reasons. Learning to be "a strong Black woman" is one of those reasons.

never sure how the word *Dad* would sound if it came out of my mouth or even the way it might feel as it slid off my tongue. Never sure what it would feel like for him to place a triple-scoop vanilla ice-cream cone in my tiny five-year-old hand, and wipe the drips off my chin with a crumpled-up napkin from his pocket, while the people who passed by whispered,

She looks just like him.

I wanted to tell him that when I think about how I grew up, the only word I tasted was *confusion* and how it seemed to tower over my teenage mind like a translucent fog full of "what ifs," "how comes," and "are you sures?" My Black mother raised me the best she could by herself, but I was sad all the time, I'm *still* sad. My East Indian-Ugandan father, not visible, never visible, I couldn't hug him like I wanted to. I couldn't hear his voice like I wanted to.

I wanted to tell him that whatever memories I had of him showed up blurry and unrecognizable, fragmented and sparse, except for the fact that we both liked massive amounts of black pepper on our over-easy eggs.

I wanted to tell him that it's okay to call me his daughter, but whether or not he saw me as such I do not know.

I didn't want to know.

I wanted to tell him that I do not look like anyone else in my family.

There's a beauty in knowing who you are.

I wanted to hide so that I wouldn't have to answer questions about my father:

Is she Black? What is she? I think she's East Indian. No, look at her hair, she's definitely not Black. Where's she from?

I wanted to tell him that even today when people ask who my father is I tell them about the eggs.

I wanted to tell him that I live in a city where everywhere you go, there are mixed people. People dipped in all three hundred and sixty-four shades of brown. People in coffee shops, bank lines, grocery stores, hair salons, libraries, crowded buses, and overbooked restaurants. And when I walk down the street with my mother, my daughter, or my cousin, I don't want to have to prove we are related by answering a series of questions, followed by a series of follow-up questions, and then long stares, and "are you sures?" ending with my own deep sighs.

I wanted to tell him—to confess—that I wasn't sure who I was back then, or now, and that I told terrible lies to avoid the questions that always came:

You've got good hair. Why do your hair up? Let your hair down. Look how long your hair is when you straighten it. Smile, your hair is beautiful. Your hair looks good against your light skin, don't you think?

I told terrible lies.

I wanted to tell him that my then eight-year-old tri-racial daughter, who's now fifteen, used to ask me why she didn't have a grandpa, and that I had no answer for her because no one had an answer for me.

I wanted to tell him that when I look into the mirror now at thirty-six, I still have no idea what I am supposed to see, and I still wonder if living in between is ever a safe place to reside.

I wanted to tell him that when people tell me I'm beautiful, it hurts for days and days.

I am a mother. I didn't want to become one.

When my daughter says she does not want to see her dad anymore, I tell her to hug her dad while she can. When she says her dad doesn't understand, I tell her to explain things to her dad while she can. When I sort through old photos of my baby daughter smiling and posing with her dad, I say to myself, she will need these someday.

I tell her to write down all the things she wanted to tell him.

Then tell him.

the cracks in the narrative represent questions, untold truths, and illogical parts of a story. These are the events that would never make sense in a world with rules. The cracks in the narrative break the rules, there's bending here too. I've been a crack in my own narrative for a long time. I didn't fit neatly into the story.

With everything I've written to date—whether poetry, prose, essay, or short story—I've written with the sole purpose to answer questions and fill space. To fill the cracks. This is no different. Kintsugi. The translation from Japanese means "golden joinery" or "to patch with gold." This technique transforms broken ceramic or china vessels into beautiful works of art and to their new life, using gold with lacquer or epoxy to enhance breaks given to the broken pottery.

In thinking about the "cracks in the narrative," the Japanese art of Kintsugi gave me a little bit of hope. Broken things can be fixed, made new, made better, beautiful again. The notion of transformation is key to healing in any sort of trauma. Transformation is essential as it relates to my childhood. I can fill those cracks with gold, if I choose to.

I still think about all the houses, the teachers, the predators, the fear. Some of these were cracks, some of these—already filled with gold.

Acknowledgements

Thank-yous

I have been working on *Dear Current Occupant* my entire life.

This was a difficult book to write for many reasons, the biggest being that I wasn't sure my memory was sharp enough to write it in the vivid way I pictured it. Four winters ago, I went back to all of the houses mentioned in this book and stood out front shivering, gripping a pen and notebook in my hand. I took notes on anything and everything I could remember. This was the first step.

So many people have been allies for me during this book's creation. First of all, thank you to Hazel and Jay Millar at BookThug for agreeing to publish *Dear Current Occupant*. Jennifer Zilm, Paul Sasges, Wayde Compton, and Mona Fertig read the very first draft—thank you. They sifted through the rubble, and still managed to offer notes and insights that made draft ten possible. My two wonderful aunts Virginia Jacobsen and Karen Knight read excerpts from drafts two and three, and their support of the work and encouragement to press on allowed me to do just that.

My good friend Jade Melnychuk toured the streets of Vancouver's Eastside with me for hours, while she expertly snapped every single photo included in this book.

Drafts eight and nine came to me like lightning, and that's because of my editor, Renée Sarojini Saklikar, who forced me to write with honesty, and to face the stories that frightened me the most. She inspired me to unlock the pieces of this story that had been rusted shut for years.

All of my friends and fellow writers at Simon Fraser University's Writer's Studio will always be essential to why and how I continue to write. Writing is indeed a solitary act, but I don't think I have ever truly been alone, thanks to the Writer's Studio.

To my "Roomies" at *Room* magazine (especially Meghan Bell, who always said, "Just ignore your email and write!")—you all rock.

The inspiring emails and phone calls from Jónína Kirton (that always seemed to come at the perfect time) prevented me from giving up on so many things, including this book.

Thank you, my lovely friends, for keeping it real and for always talking me out of giving up. Samantha deVries-Hofman and Jessica Kent—that means you!

"like a lion in the trees" could not have been written without the back-and-forth "fragmenting" in the tiny notebook I shared with David Hallihan. Let us never stop writing! I hope we finish our chapbook soon.

My biggest thank-you is for my love, Richard Riordan, who from day one made me feel like every story I had to tell was worthy of breathing air, and worthy of being in print. For this I am eternally grateful. "lay your head on my pillow" is for him.

To my brother David Knight and my momma, Sandra Knight: everything we've been through made us all who we are today. I am grateful for every difficult day… We are still here and the three of us are made stronger because of it.

Notes

I would like to acknowledge the influences and inspiration of Dionne Brand, Audre Lorde, and Jamaica Kincaid, whose work helped me to fully see and appreciate the scope of my own words. The final piece of this book, "mama, you need to know some things," was first written as a short erasure poem inspired by and in response to Jamaica Kincaid's beautiful book *Autobiography of My Mother*. It was then expanded into a reflective essay meant to "mirror" the last piece in the prologue, "mama."

Older versions of "lay your head on my pillow" and "never sure how the word *Dad*" were originally published under different titles on mixedrootsstories.com.

"Miss Parker" and an older version of "mama, you need to know some things" (under a different title) were both published first in the *Maynard*.

Chelene Knight was born in Vancouver, and is currently the managing editor of *Room Magazine*. A graduate of the Writer's Studio at SFU, Chelene has been published in various Canadian and American literary magazines. Her debut book, *Braided Skin*, was published in 2015. *Dear Current Occupant* is her second book.

PHOTO CREDIT: CHELENE KNIGHT

COLOPHON

Manufactured as the first edition of *Dear Current Occupant* in the spring of 2018 by Book*hug.

Distributed in Canada by the Literary Press Group: www.lpg.ca
Distributed in the US by Small Press Distribution: www.spdbooks.org
Shop online at www.bookthug.ca

BOOK
PRODUCTION
WAR ECONOMY
STANDARD

Edited for the press by Renée Saklikar
Type + design by Carleton Wilson
Cover by Gareth Lind / Lind Design
Copy edited by Stuart Ross